GW01085755

Dreaming at Noon

poems

Michael G. Donkin

Finishing Line Press
Georgetown, Kentucky

Dreaming at Noon

ACKNOWLEDGMENTS

The author thanks the editors of the following journals for publishing some
of these poems: *Majority Post; Bangalore Review*

Publisher: Leah Huete de Maines
Editor: Christen Kincaid
Cover Art: *Sita*, by Odilon Redon
Author Photo: Cristina Farella
Cover Design: Elizabeth Maines McCleavy

Order online: www.finishinglinepress.com
also available on amazon.com

Author inquiries and mail orders:
Finishing Line Press
PO Box 1626
Georgetown, Kentucky 40324
USA

Table of Contents

to Cristina

I want to sleep near the sky like the astrologers …

Baudelaire

Cycle

A sphere did not receive love,
It grew thin and became a circle.

A pyramid did not receive death,
It grew thin, it became a triangle.

A flower did not receive sun-light,
It grew thin, it died.

And when it died, it turned into a sphere,
It became the earth.

And when the earth did not receive love,
It grew thin and became the sky.

Reason

A star made life
With earth, the life

Form that resulted
Appeared as a blend

Of sun and earth.
Blossoms thus live

In the ground and
Radiate as the sun.

Looking

When you look at the sun
You'll see a red or yellow or a white kind of circle or disc
In the midst of a blue or grey or white but never a black sky.
The sky is black only when the sun isn't in it.

Almost everyone knows the sun isn't visible then.
This is because at night the sun is underground, hidden—

If you'd ever like to behold the sun in a pitch-black sky
You would have to find a way of penetrating the sky
So as to make it to the other side.
But be careful: on the other side is the land of Titans.

They are not like us.
They're spheres, perfect in roundness and shocking in size
That float eternally in a place without air.

Forgetting

Why can I remember dreams
But no event in the waking days I have lived?
Each day for me functions as a dream
I have repressed,
I am sure I'm not asleep now
Still I'm sure I will fail to remember writing this.

Each morning I am reborn into the light
Of the gloriously banal,
As an exile that must draw on those
Manifold experiences
From the strange and delirious hallucinations
Had in the other country.
—

Many are surprised to hear that my dreams in aggregate
Grant me the same knowledge others accumulate
Living out their lives in the sun.

While it's true that if I do not sleep I won't die
It's also true that I will have no life.

Certainty

But you should learn to wake up in your dreams,
Controlling dreams is preferable to experiencing
Them unconsciously…
You must be active, not passive,
I should be the dictator of my dreams
For then I could do anything I pleased. . .
To them I say I would never try to control any dream
No matter how unsettling.

I prefer to be dumb like a real-life dictator,
Fearful of being hunted down,
Humiliated and hung upside down in the town square.
The unconscious dream is preferable,
And so much so, that each morning I wake up
I am overcome with a horrible sadness
At having awoken from the illusion

That death should be avoided at all costs.
It makes me most sad of all when I am forced back
To the horrible awareness that being not dead
Means being awake inside of a dream
From which each of us
Awakens when he is dead.

Essence

I lived in that home
Till I became in every
Sense the home itself;
At last there was no
Difference between my
Self and it; meanwhile
The house managed
To become in every
Sense me: it lived
Inside this body and
Soul as my essence . .

Ends

Each day I awaken
And pursue objectives.

I go to sleep when it is over
Only to reawaken.

These so-called days
And nights are curious.

They lead to more
Days and nights.

Maybe there is no
Goal in itself but the sun

And only maps
Which lead to other maps

And every day is pursued
For its own sake.

I Do Not Wish to Be Complete

I do not wish to be complete; a self-sufficient person.
I love being what I am: incomplete. It allows me to suffer
And have enlivening romance with existence.

I'm no angel, complete from the beginning.
I contemplate the world, and so I excite myself.
I worship the sun each day and the stars each night.

Although I know the rest of me is out there
I have little interest in finding it.
Perhaps in the future, when I'm not able to look

And piece together the mysterious parts of the world anymore
I'll go out and recover the rest of 'me,'
But this would mean that my search has stopped.

Dreamed Poem

The dream calls each night like lethal seawater
Calls to the mouth of someone who has been
Out to sea without water for days

Death calls like the body of one who dances
Before a traveler who for years has not seen another body

…Each individual is alone, each seeks oblivion

Every being is a traveler that yearns
For a sense of understanding in an unholy city
Wherein nobody speaks the same language

Every infant was exiled at birth and sleeps to return to its origin,
In the end each will perish and drink from the same source
Until oblivion calls for its new life to begin.

Following

In the city, I saw someone I thought
I knew.
Maybe I did know them. From behind
I thought it might be they.
I followed them for many blocks,
Never quite catching up.
It seemed the faster I walked,
The faster they would walk in turn.

I kept on, neither becoming surer
Nor less sure this person was the one I thought I knew.
For days and nights
I kept on,
Following them to the edge of the city,
Through the countryside and finally to the sea.
Yes, I even crossed the sea in pursuit of this one
Who may not have been the one I had known

Whose ambiguity I was now used to—
I began to feel affection toward this person
Whose back I had become so familiar with.
If they were to turn around,
Confirming or disconfirming my suspicion,
I think I might have dropped dead, having grown
So used to their ambiguity,
  Which had become a sort of dear friend to me.

Impossible Wish

I think I prefer it infinitely to be out west. For here the sun sets into the mouth of the sea. And the steam made by this meeting makes the clouds, which soar high up overhead.

And when the sky is full of them, clouds, they burst…until the sea is filled again with water… Then, as the moon rises, its light swirls the darkness and the sea around—it fills me with joy to watch and understand.

Yet… as the sun rises out of the sea, it means that we're back in the east. And I know that this is the matter with the west, and I have a sudden need to be in the east at the same time as the west, which is not possible.

A Concept

The athlete awoke at dawn to perform his ritual . . .

As he lifted his sack, a sack of stones, he heard the voice of the sea—
It awaited him beyond the cliffs! . .
"I love the sea," he sang,
"I love you, even if you have no purpose
Besides giving human beings pleasure, and allowing them to dream
    spectacular dreams!"

In response, the sea spoke. . "And you too are beautiful, human,
Which in itself is enough for me,
For the sea, more than anyone else, relishes beauty,
I have no purpose!"

When the athlete completed the ritual, he lay by the sea, and bathed
beneath the sun
Which had already made possible everything.

"I am the sun," it spoke—
"I give as well as take life,
And that is all that I shall ever do.
I can conceive of no better purpose, than the purpose
Which I have always had—this purpose I have never questioned. . .
What is beauty?
What is this thing, the sea?   What is athlete?

But someday I too will perish.
What is it, sun?
What is this concept which you call purpose?"

The athlete lay by the sea,
But he did not think at all of the sun's speech.
     . . .
There he dreamed that he was a sack of stones.

G. tridens

G. tridens, a fruit fly, has what looks to be a kind of diptych painted upon its wings. On each wing is an ant. Each has six legs, antennae, a thorax, a tapered abdomen, and a head. We may wonder how any mere bug could have adapted with such perverse specificity and in such fine detail. We wonder if *G. tridens* is aware, to any extent, of what it is, or indeed what it has. Is *G. tridens* deserving in some way of credit for its ingenious markings? We wonder if it should be credited for these, perhaps because we have to—we must—confer accolades somewhere. It becomes clear enough, though, in the end just how incidental *G. tridens* is to its own exquisiteness, and that *G. tridens* is not truly the protagonist of this tale. The true protagonist here is nature, just as the true story here is of nature. But nature, like *G. tridens*, is a cipher, for the word "nature" signifies nothing anymore, because nature is everything and is therefore nothing. But what should happen if a new type of pelican emerged from the sky or the depths and announced itself with the *Epic of Gilgamesh* tattooed all over its bill? Would that change our minds? Would it change our souls?

Disappearance

There are vague accounts of a book recorded along the walls of an Assyrian temple built in the shape of a cone. To read it, the worshipper had to enter at the base of the temple and, facing the single, continuous wall, moved along its perimeter, ascending imperceptibly. Thousands of worshippers entered each year, on the high holy days. Together they chanted—each from a different place in the text—taking over that of the worshipper who went before him as he spiraled upwards, infinitely…or so it seemed. Over time, each grew smaller until he was swallowed by the inevitable nothingness at the apex of the cone.

Event

All words were taken
And locked inside the sun

And they became hot till
They were soft and glowed red

They melted into one sign
Which held every thing every idea

(This new thing was black…)
And the sun projected it

For the people to see
Who could no longer read.

Together
The people sang and wept

Image

When we are not alive,
All is as it is
But there is no sun,
No moon at night,
No stars, no breathing,
No murmurs, no clouds;
All is white
In the day, all is
White at night;

There is no sea,
No wind, no trees,
No horizon,
No thoughts,
No writing, no time—

Still our mouths
Are to be held

In the shape of an 'o,'
Our eyes opened very wide
As though surprised.

Artifice

1.
Poetry enables humanity to envisage and imitate the act of creation
Out of an interplay of the elements found in nature.
2.
The poet makes connections, the poet assumes a divine origin for all:
The sun and earth; the fields and sea
3.
Are as clay to the poet, who is the maker, the artificer.
Poetry envisions those processes by which phenomena may have
    come into existence…
4.
Humanity is made from the clay, it is said.
The origin of the universe now accounted for, the poet ascribes many
    other creations
5.
To the deities, who are themselves poets
For whom humanity offers a plenitude of sacrifice, mirroring the
    plenitude of creation…
6.
From the beginning, poetry and religion nourished each other in
    reciprocal fashion.
And though a poem is composed of lines, its form is a circle.

Dialogue

THE WATER-GIVER:
Like the 'I,' our 'Sun' appears
Greater than other lights;
There are innumerable stars
As large, or larger,
Equally deserving
Of the name 'Sun.'
Around the 'I'
Are innumerable
'I's' with equal gravity.

THE LION:
What do you mean?

Song

At the seed
Of a day
Is the pinkest
Of light
Ah it is me!
I am the sun!
O
I am the sun!
The moon,
A mirror
Everybody else is
Quite
Wonderful

Yes
When
I look into a soul
I capture death.
O
I am the light
And my death
Was triangle.

Walk with Me

The god sheds a tear:
It's the white pyramid
Under a star-studded sky.

But
Walk with me beyond
The blanched hedges
Where the bees swarm.
The night is fragrant.

I Feel

The unconscious
In all which is
In birds in insects
In snow-capped
Mountains
In the sun and sea
In the flavor of wind
In an old sighing
Bridge of gray mist

I can sense
A vast near
Limitless suffering
In all which isn't
Then at once I am
Left with a savage
Compulsion
Toward your body

A Poem

I opened my eyes
And saw a tree.
It was beautiful and green.

I cut it down
And made paper,
I wrote of when
I had seen that tree.

I closed my eyes
And heard
A buzzing in the glade.

A bee!
I was not afraid.

I knew it was
Making honey.

I let my eyes open,
Hoping to write of it.
But I did not have paper.

I wrote a poem
In my head
But cannot remember
What it said.

Poem

Bee of desire you gather pollen
Since you have wings and a knife

You defile the laws which are sweet
In the shape of blossoms

I can't stand having fingers of mist
I need to catch you in the air.

Comparisons

Some are dominant within
Their subjective self.
Relatively, they lack competence
In terms of what they put out into the world.
They cannot communicate
Or relate with others as easily
As perhaps they should.
Others have little inside them
But are proficient in terms of their
Social and intellectual competence.
In the end however,
It is better to be a yellow flower.

Birds

My twin and I had always communicated with the greatest ease. A mere glance was often sufficient to convey the desire for movement, animals, rain. We awoke invariably in the tower of the gods utterly refreshed and without humor; afternoons we spent in the city, holidays in the provinces. To see her float everlastingly toward the horizon, across the vast green surface of the dream, reinforced the simple reason why she was the one for me. It was her radius which first attracted me, all those millennia ago, in Antarctica, where diamonds were plentiful as they are in Africa. The skulls—not of this planet—piled at the entrance to her steel labyrinth were the first sign something was distinctly without precedent. She was more an idea than a body. And I, a mere point in time, in need of understanding and companionship. The train would pass behind the world, concealed, but for its mysterious scream. Each minute it returned from its tour of the islands, dragging behind it a net of fish, lobsters, dolphins which were to be stretched and liquefied under the ground, then administered to her center. My other understood everything about me, despite my deficit. Her wholeness threw into relief my metaphysical incompleteness. She was inevitably perfectly complete, without me. Hence she was imperious, a fixture of reality, a sort of originary fluid through which I animated my feelings in physical form. Birds flew, and it was because they were afraid of her depths.

Earth

I wished to bury the earth.
I began to dig a hole.
I would dig a hole in which to bury it.
I dug and dug.
My hole had to be
At least the size of the earth
If the earth was to fit inside.
When I had finished digging my hole
As big as the earth, it dawned on me:
I had dug up the entire earth.
No longer was there
Any place to put it.
I floated away.

The Tower

To defy the gods
I commissioned a
Tower to be built,
Which would be
Terrific enough
To penetrate the sky itself,
It was assuredly
The greatest ever built.
But, like myself,
Owing to its bulk,
The tower would,
In time, sink back
Into the earth, the
Mud, its rightful origin:
While it is no longer
Known to human
Kind, since nobody uses
Or admires it now, my
Tower, in spite of all, is
The deepest ever built.

The Home

In my time I have known
Great painters great poets

Great philosophers and
Great pornographers,

And still I have not known
A great architect.

Introduce him to me,
And I am bound to inform him

Of a huge sadness . .
Let him make a house for it.

Account

I have ninety persons in my employ.
I have sixty-two fools and thirty-five maple trees,
I have twenty-four dogs and forty-three goats.
I have sixty-two wives,
Three tropical birds, four sons, four thousand concubines,
Two hundred beautiful daughters
And a human man who just sits here without saying a word
In my palace courtyard.
I think that he contrives to undercut my very livelihood
And reap all the benefits.
He is excellent company all the same.
Sometimes I think I would murder for this person.
Other times I think I would lay down my life for him.
He is my soul's shadow.
He is that which gives firmness
To my vaguest contours if I stroll in perfect darkness.
He is the one human unafraid
To defy my severest logic
When I am near to sleep at night.
He pollutes my thought-flickers.
He violates the drinking water with his mellow chanting.

The Creation

When they buried me they put all my statues
In the very ditch in which I was to be put.
Next they put in my estate,
Then my eagles, followed by my horses.
Then my telephone, my raiment, and my whips,
Then my sons and my nephews.
Next they put the soldiers in that ditch, too.

They put my dogs, then my telescope, my bicycle,
And my favorite eating chair,
My cushion, my geographers, my cousins,
My skulls, my best singers.
They lowered in my favorite books of verse,
My bathtub, my livestock, my precious stones.
They lowered in my arms and my legs
And folded me in thirds.
They lowered in my chamber,
My fortress, my helicopter,
My bees, my armies, my scents, my rakes.

They gently put in my stomach, my genitals
And all the beauty of this realm
And the realm itself.
And then the cosmos and the forms
And the gods and all of time
And all the love
That was meant for me and me alone.
From here it would start anew.

ADDITIONAL ACKNOWLEDGEMENTS

Many thanks to the following for reading my work, your inspiration and moral support, in no particular order: Wesley Mattingly, Mariana Louis, Bruce Gardner, David Michael Mullins, Derek Thomas Dew, Julia Nemirovskaya, B Lee-Harrison Aultman, Alex Modlin, Dan Hersh, Vanessa Petrea, Odile DeWar, Adam Pogioli, Arvind Binnie Katti, Jiesha Stephens, Teresa Hernández, Martin Franzini, James Barton, Emily Zhao, Murad Jalilov, Aida Vahidova, David Greenwood, James Donovan, Patricia Ruland, Meredith Mullins, Ian Galloway, Sherence de Jongh, Brother Sebek, Ariane Verticordia, Brian Reeder, Philipp Luft, Eli Ari, Larry Balanovsky, Nadia Vikulina, Marcin Rusinkiewicz, Gonzalo Fernandez, Aisha Maria, Qi Tai Wong, Ben Merriman, Chad McCarty, Tyler Olsen, Dusty, Nicole Brock, Genie Hulyer, Jean Diamond, Hansi Golightly, my parents, family, and many others

Michael G. Donkin was born in Washington, DC in 1984.